Thoughts Of A

Spiritual Queen

By Kelilah Lynette

DEDICATION

To My Heavenly Father and My Mother, for walking beside me, supporting me with my life choices, and sticking by me through the ups and downs. They are and forever will be my motivation, my rock and my shield. Last and not least my lovely readers, I hope to inspire and touch every soul who reads my poems. We are connected through my words you see my life and you explore my mind through my poetry.

MY POETRY LIST

 *KING AND QUEEN*

 *LIFE OVER DEATH*

 *DEAR HEAVENLY FATHER*

 *GOOD MAN*

 *WHEN I SEE YOU*

 *PAIN*

 *WHEN I LOOK AT YOU*

SOUL TOUCH

OPEN YOUR EYES

I CAN MAKE YOU FEEL

ESSENCES OF A WOMAN

PATIENCE

SOUL MATE

MISSING YOU

WHO SAID

BLIND VISION

TWO PEOPLE ONE SOUL

LOOKS CAN BE DECEIVING

WE ALL HAVE A STORY

LOYALTY

ACKNOWLEDGMENTS

I would like to express my gratitude to My Heavenly Father, thank you for all things and everything. Without you in my life, my faith in you, and my gift you blessed me with, I don't know where I'll be today.

You have given me the power to believe in my passion, purpose, and to pursue my dreams.

As I gather this material together I see how amazing my gift of writing is.

I am forever grateful and humble enough to accept all challenges that this may bring.

I want to acknowledge my family, friends, and my readers. I am grateful for your love, support, encouragement, and feedback. I would not have the courage to express my thoughts, my views, and my passion, through words on a paper. By me putting together this book has allowed me to share with you all, some of the things that I love, and enjoy in life, I thank you for that.

Life isn't worth living if you have no purpose or destination.

Kelilah ♥

King And Queen

What is a Queen?

Without her King, what is a king without his queen?

The two of them gives each other balance, love, fulfillment, and completion

A bond so strong no one can break it.

Love so deep it goes on like time, it continues forever.

He protects her and loves her and she holds him down and never leaves his side.

When you see him you see her, and when you see her you see him.

There reflection of each other is a beautiful a gift no money can buy.

When you see them you see The Heavenly Father in them.

There love is so strong so powerful they don't need to speak it you see it, these very words love.

Kelilah ♥

Life over Death

Life over death, spirit over flesh

This life we living glorifies bad over good.

And they hate good and love bad

Your faith, your actions and your love

For The Heavenly Father and his Son

Will be tested

Love over evil, anytime and any day

Nothing in this world and of this flesh is worth going to hell for.

You must love and give with your whole heart, have faith.

And give with your whole heart, eyes, mind, thoughts, and actions.

Know that you are chosen to be Sons and Daughters of and Almighty King Power.

To the chosen people no one can take your promise your Covenant we must fight to the end.

Fight for your position fight for your white robe.

If that means to give up all sinful things and pleasures of this world anything that doesn't have anything to do with holiness and our Almighty Father you must do it.

Will u ride or die for him will you give up so much for that promise?

Who will stand up as his Sons and Daughters of and Almighty King who will say I give my all and my whole heart for him.

I tell you who His Chosen People Life over Death Spirit Over Flesh.

Kelilah♥

Dear Heavenly Father

I want to start off by saying how much you mean to me

I love you unconditionally.

You mean more to me than you can imagine.

You care about me and love me for me you understand me.

You show me things that only you can explain.

You are the only real father I've ever had in my life.

Your love, grace, mercy, understanding, compassion, towards me and your

Children you are what a true Father is suppose to be.

I'm so blessed and grateful to know you love you and follow all that I am

suppose to do as your daughter.

You show me what it is to love unconditionally, patients, understanding,

Wisdom, Knowledge, Forgiveness, Caring, Humbleness, growth to be a better

me.

Every day to honor respect others and see what life really is, perfection only

Comes from you, we were born to sin born to die; flaws are a part of us.

You are the best spiritual Father anyone can ask for.

When someone say who's my Father I say you, when one ask who I love I say

You, when one ask who will I give my life to and die for I say you.

When one says, who do I honor, respect, and worship, I say you.

When I look in the water, the sand, the dirt, the sun, the moon, the stars, the trees, the animals, and my brother and sisters in this world I see you're perfection his chosen people and all I can say is Thank You for Choosing Me.

Kelilah♥

Good Man

What is a good man?

I was raised fatherless but I've gained a Heavenly Father in the process

From what I've seen and experienced I know exactly what one is.

A good man is one who shows appreciation in all things small or big; He values love, respect, loyalty, family and most of all God.

His reflection is of Our Heavenly Father and Christ someone who shows devotion in others and within himself.

He is a blessing from up above and a blessing in a heart of his wife. His love is so rare every word he speaks is music to the ear, every walk he makes is like his walking on clouds.

He is the definition of greatness, and unconditional love, passion, royalty.

Your Royalty picks up your crown you are royal, royal because you are the closes thing to and angel.

You are the image of God you are the son of a king and you where made to be just that.

You're destined to be greater then what society portrays you to be, don't let anyone take your crown. Best gift you can give a woman is your 100% nothing less.

What's a king without his queen just a prince ready to be crowned. A good women like myself will honor them and love them until death do us part.

For all the good men you are loved and appreciated you are royalty.

Kelilah♥

When I See You

When I see you I see the reflection of a good man.

When I'm in your presents I feel like I'm in the presents of a king.

When you speak your words is smooth like butter, and when you look at me

I see my reflection.

When you touch me I feel it from my head to my toes

You make my flesh get Goosebumps.

You make my spirit sing, you make my soul cry out for you.

I never knew how much I needed you

Until I open my eyes and saw you.

The look you gave me was a look only someone made for me would give me

I can finally breathe, I can finally enjoy life with you, and I can finally create memories that will last for a lifetime.

I can't stop smiling I can't stop thanking The Creator for you.

As I look at you all I can think of is my prayers have finally been answered.

I cannot wait to share your last name

As I close my eyes to see if this is a dream.

When I reopen them I realize

This is a dream I want this dream to be my reality.

So don't wake me up until this is my reality

Because I want to start living and without you I feel like I am dying.

Kelilah♥

Pain

Pain is a painful suffering or discomfort one feels in its body, spirit, and soul
we all experience it we all live it.

So powerful it becomes you it takes over your every essence.

When we cry and angel cries when we hurt and angel hurts they can feel

What we feel.

Pain is as real as love is and it will take over your very essence if you let it.

Pain is short term and long term if u let it

Pain is the opposite of love don't let it control you and become you.

Overcome the pain like an over comer does smile a little, laugh a Little

Harder, give to those in need, be a better you and most of all enjoy your life.

Each and every day is grateful to be able to breathe, walk, eat, and love, live a

little longer, you have a chance to be happy, loving, loyal, generous,

To be a better sibling, better parent, better child, better spouse, a better you.

Pain will not define you it will not beat you down and overpower you we will show pain that love and happiness wins.

It will answer at our darkest hours and our lighter hours when we needed it the most.

Keep pushing to be happy, keep pushing to love, and keep pushing to be a light to others, by doing so will always come with rewards seen and unseen.

Kelilah♥

When I Look At You

Created For My Soul mate♥

When I look at u I see hope I see unconditional love, patients, understanding, caring, affectionate.

And this is what I want, need and longing for

To grow old with my life partner, my, best friend, my husband.

Everything we do is partnership nobody or no one can come between us

I want the now, and the forever, I want I and Love and you.

I want the kisses and the hugs and the I miss you.

I want the unconditional love that you will give to me

Something like our grandparents had through thick and thin.

With the up and downs not the break ups or divorce or the mistress or misters not the hate u and I regret being with you.

Call me crazy but I want the true love the love that is so real that you can feel and see it.

It will feel so good that u don't even feel like you on earth in a different realm.

So heavenly further then cloud 9 when on our own planet made for just me and you

Can this be you can this be us the way you will make me feel can this be true.

We are not each other's first but I am planning and preparing to be your last

Always giving praises to The Most High who blessed us.

Kelilah♥

Soul Touch

I don't break hearts I soul touch.

I want you to see me and feel me with one look.

I want you to remember my name every time our souls touch.

When I touch you I want you to be open like a token.

When I say I want you I want you to feel it and need me

When I say I love you I want your soul and spirit to understand me and love me.

My love is so real so unconditional I got men lined up trying to be my king.

I'm waiting on my king like a soul ready to be joined at last.

I'm so ready that I dream him, and think of him, I can almost see him almost feel him.

How I imagine him is an indescribable feeling like souls becoming one

So indescribable, unchangeable, irreplaceable

Our souls will understand each other.

Our thoughts will be one; our words will flow together like music notes.

Our love and our journey will be and inspiration to others

To not give up on love it is out there and it's for everyone.

Our Creator made someone for everyone no one is left out everyone will have that special one designed for them.

His power and love will reflect through us.

Kelilah♥

Open Your Eyes

Every day I wake up I see and hear death; life is becoming harder to live,

But only people I see affected is those who have faith in the creator

Yet those people eyes are wide shut to the facts.

The scriptures in the bible are being revealed to us right before our eyes.

Just take a step back, take a deep breath and open all 3 eyes and you will see.

What I see, people yelling change, equal rights, reparations, freedom, respect.

Yelling and marching for respect, justice, and for answers, still no results.

Why is that I'll tell you why we live in a world run by malevolent spirits.

In order to see any progress as a whole we must return to

The Creator of all things

Because through him all things will happen for us, until you get back to The

Creator, Our Heavenly Father all those prayers will fall on deaf ears.

Turn to him get on your knees and seek him, if you don't change your actions,

lifestyle, you can't expect your prayers to be heard.

Chose life, over death, chose good, over evil, chose positive, over negative.

Kelilah♥

I can make you feel

I want to make you feel good physically, mentally, spiritually, emotionally,

I want your thoughts of me to blow your mind.

I want my name and the way I speak to you give you chills, I want my lips

Against yours, I want your heart to skip a beat when I'm in your presents.

I want you to experience unconditional love as my king.

I want to build with you, I want to support your every move, I want to love you

with my whole being not just my heart, and I will be by your side.

I will be your number one fan in everything you do there's no me without you.

As your queen I will submit myself to you because you are the definition of a

head/husband, I can only thank The Most High for answering my prayers.

When he brought you in my life, every day I feel rich of love, rich of respect,

rich of loyalty, rich of love, rich of your presents, you make me feel rich

spiritually.

My spirit wants for nothing, my heart lacks for nothing, my mind lacks of nothing, and you feed me with wisdom, and knowledge, which is beyond words.

Together we are powerful and without each other we are weak.

They say you reap what you sew and I am reaping and sewing my blessings from my obedience to The Creator.

Kelilah♥

Essence of a Woman

Soft lips soft skin scent smells so good you want to taste it,

I'm on his mind he sees me everywhere he goes.

What he wouldn't do to get a taste, a moment a second he want this forever

It looks so good you want to touch it.

Feels so good he doesn't want to leave it, could I be his angel sent from heaven

Or could I be his good luck charm.

Whatever it is I want him to miss me, love me, kiss me, keep me, make love to me until we tap out and do it all over again.

He so hooked he got my name on everything loving so good

I got him saying my name.

Kelilah is the name remember it never forget it

I am the blessing in your life not the curse.

Not the headache not pain not drama not the regret

I am the one who will change your life.

Spiritually, physically, emotionally, mentally

I am the blessing

Kelilah♥

Patience

They say patience is a virtue

But how much patience do we really have, we are living in a world where patience seems forever.

Time is speeding up, and things are growing fast world is changing, the population is growing, and evil has increased and the good has decreased.

The saints are praying more, but the sinners are still committing more sins,

The people eyes are still shut, while the ones with their eyes wide open.

Is still falling victim to this society to their environment, so I say pray quicker,

Choose good over evil, find love now because the years aren't promised, continue to do right and choose The Creator, and get right while you can.

Live life to the fullest because nothing good last forever

In this corrupt world Patience is what's needed now and forever

Kelilah♥

Soul mate

Life with your soul mate is beautiful you become one with one another.

You complete each other's sentences you stick together like glue.

When you see her you see him when you see him you see her.

The love they share is unbreakable, uncontrollable, unconditional unstoppable, no one can get between them.

They love each other so much they cannot and will not live without each other

There happiness and needs and wants comes first.

There's nothing they wouldn't do for each other

You can't put a price on happiness or love once you experience that.

Never let it go and never take it for granted cherish your blessing

Many look for it and want it but so little receives it.

Kelilah♥

Missing You

I miss you when I wake up I miss you when I go to sleep

Every thought and imagination is of you.

I can't wait to meet you when I write these poems I think of you and day dream of you.

Every minute I'm awake I think of how our life will be how our first day of meeting will be.

Will you know I'm your wife soon as we meet will I know you're my husband when I meet you.

Will you love me unconditionally, will you understand me, and will you trust me.

Will I be enough for you, will you ride or die for me, and will you fight for me.

I will love you I won't let anyone take your place.

I will fight for you, I will understand you, I will trust you, and protect you

Be supportive, I will fulfill your every need, I'll do anything so I won't lose you

Because I love you and you're worth it you can be anything to them but to me.

You're perfect I'll fight for you I'm right for you I'm here on purpose not by mistake.

Missing you is like the stars missing the sky like the sun missing the moon

Like a tree missing its roots, ocean missing the water.

I pray for you every day, and when I meet you the stars will be bright for us the sun will shine brighter for us love will be in the air for us

Oh what a life.

Kelilah♥

Who Said

Who said makeup and fake hair defines you.

So please take it off so he can see the real you.

Whoever told u that stuff defines society's beauty move over and let us naturals show you real beauty.

It's so skin deep you can feel it, it's so bright you can't see it It's so unique it's graceful.

A woman's crown is her sacred place so precious so marvelous no one should touch it.

That's why when you pray or prophesies you must cover it. You're natural crown shows self love, dignity, strength, breaking the curses.

Being the chain breaker the dogma that's been instilled since birth. Who told you to stop loving the way God made you?

Who told u to stop embracing what God already put his paint brush on?

Who told you that beauty was flawless and made up to be something you're not. Just like any scar it is made to heal just like beauty it is made to be revealed not hidden away.

Who told you to stop loving yourself; you must love you first before you can love another.

Who ever told you your not beautiful send him to God and tell him he made no mistakes when he made you.

Kelilah♥

Blind Vision

Blind vision living in a world where no one can see you

Blind and utterly destroyed by the lack of knowledge that spills through.

They trying to wipe out Gods chosen people, it's in their nature to do evil

As in the beginning also shall it be in the end.

Only time heals, racism, and white supremacy, is only temporary

Living now has to be worse than in the past when I look at this place I am so disgusted and sad filled with sorrow filled with disgrace.

How could this be heaven on earth it's looking more like hell on earth.

Every day I wake up I pray for forgiveness, mercy, sin, lust, love protection, shield to guard us from these demons that is set loose upon this earth.

I pray for peace and for others only God knows how much we need him every move I make and people I see blind vision written all on their face.

It's like I am looking at the end but still hoping for a brighter future.

I must be dreaming or being optimistic.

It's like I am looking for love but it's in my face just waiting to be found.

Hoping for longevity of this world but I know the end of it is my face.

Kelilah♥

Two People One Soul

Looking for the right one is like looking for a needle in a haystack.

Looking in all the wrong places and finding all the wrong things.

You realize what you're looking for could be right under your nose

Like the flowers you smell in the spring.

That person could be looking for you might even be looking at you while praying for you, thinking about you, right now at this moment.

Could it be that your soul mate was made the same time when

The creator made you.

Two spirits to enter this earth this atmosphere to one day join together and be together as one in this lifetime.

It was written in the sky, the stars, and the moon, the sun, the clouds

She will be so perfect so awesome only the one can see through her soul.

He will be so perfect so amazing his imperfection become your perfection.

Someone made just for you thought of just for you how lucky how blessed one would be to experience life with someone who spirit was made to join with your spirit.

Who will be with you forever no one can change what's created just for you.

When you meet your soul mate you will then know and experience true love in its entirety and its true essence.

Everything they do you love, everything they see you see, everything they feel you feel, everything they say you understand, everything about them is perfection at its finest.

O how life would be to spend the rest of it with your other half.

Kelilah♥

Looks can be deceiving

Looks can be deceiving and words can be misleading

A heart can be broken, or cherished.

Words can cut like a knife; Actions can speak volumes louder then speakers.

Trust can be gain and lost at the same time.

Justice can prevail, just like these curses can be up lifted off us.

Lift up my spirit lift up my sins; I am just a young lioness trying to live righteous, but all I see is darkness all around me.

I want to be a light in this dark world, I want my words to touch your soul, and make your mind race.

My thoughts are only an expression of me, if you can understand my thoughts and the way I think you already gained access to my spirit.

My spirit is love, light, greatness,

All praises to The Creator for creating my essence.   Kelilah♥

We All Have a Story

We all have a story a mission and purpose

What we do with ourselves will determine the outcome of our destiny.

If I knew that life on this earth won't make it past 20 yrs my purpose and goals has to be complete.

I was Raised by a single mother I know struggle.

I fell in love once and hurt again and again I am learning to accept that I am different than most.

I am learning to accept my flaws and my sins begging for forgiveness every day.

I am learning to understand the cards I was dealt with and the unexplained.

I'm learning to cope with the struggle in this world praying for my sins and others daily.

I am praying for our struggles and hoping it will all go away one day.

I am praying for the love that we all need praying, for the fatherless because I am one.

We all need that guidance, protection, love, support, that a father should live and die to give to his children.

I am praying for humbleness, understanding, knowledge, wisdom, guidance, protection, and unconditional love.

But I realize the only way our prayers will be answered is by being that and more.

Kelilah♥

Loyalty

Loyalty everyone wants it and everyone expects it

But so little give it.

What is it? Loyalty is a quality of being loyal to someone or something

So rare so unique but so little respect it and anticipate it.

I live for it I am it; I will demand it in every aspect of my being.

What will one do for loyalty? Can you see it, can you feel it, and can you be it

When I see it I shall honor it, loyalty is so scarce in this time.

But it should be wanted and needed like one wants and needs Love.

Once you experience loyalty it becomes your every essence. It is true and genuine no money can buy; it will make those with pride shamefaced those with egos humble.

Kelilah♥

ABOUT THE AUTHOR

❖   *I was born in Yonkers, New York by parents of Jamaican origin. I have lived in New York, Houston Texas, and now living in Florida. I am 25 born May 28, 1990 my first passion is poetry and my first love are for The Most High also known as The Heavenly Father and my second love would have to be ice-cream. ☺*

❖   *My Inspiration of writing has come from the love and passion I have for poetry. Also with the help Of Our Heavenly Father and mother and great poets as motivation.*

❖   *I started off writing all my poems down in high school. Then I advanced to putting my poems on word press. And a good friend of mine told me about createspace.com and I decided to publish my first poetry book. I am so ecstatic I feel like I accomplished a huge mild stone and I am looking forward to this journey.*

❖   *Thank you for all your support and love*

Sincerely Kelilah Lynette

www.ingramcontent.com/pod-product-compliance
Lightning Source LLC
Chambersburg PA
CBHW040345060426
42445CB00029B/6